Yoni Massage

Advanced Techniques To Sexually Please A Woman

Francisco Bujan

www.vitalcoaching.com

Tantric sex – Online

http://vitalcoaching.com/tantricsex.htm

Tantric sex – Coaching

Check this link:

http://vitalcoaching.com/coaching.htm

Yoni Massage

Yoni massage - Clitoris stimulation - Advanced techniques

This is another core advanced technique especially for guys (or women if you and your tantric sex partner are both females).

Women will often be purely clitoridian.

This means that they orgasm mainly through clitoris stimulation.

You can stimulate the clitoris with your finger or hand. You can use your tongue and lips.

You can as well of course stimulate her clitoris through intercourse.

Now, when you have intercourse and want to increase stimulation on her clitoris, you do that by pressing your pubic bone against hers a bit stronger.

You don't focus on the ebb and flow of your penetration but rather increase the pressure between your two pubic bones.

This by itself stimulates her clitoris.

This is what often makes a woman come.

Try it! You will be amazed if you never observed that simple trick.

While you press your pubic bone against hers, you can engage either in circular movements or in and out movements.

Both types of moves will massage her clitoris while stimulating her internally as well.

Now, many women prefer vaginal stimulation.

In other terms, they prefer the feeling of penetration and get aroused by the stimulation of their G-spot.

The best way to find out what she likes is to ask.

"If you have the choice between a wet finger stroking your clitoris, my tongue and penetration, which one do you prefer?"

Yes! You can engage in sexual communication and find out what she would do if she was by herself.

Next point: stroking her clitoris!

There is a hood or skin covering her clitoris.

For best results, you can pull back that skin with your thumb and stroke her clitoris with your index finger.

You see this tiny rose mount which is like a tiny wet seed.

The clitoris has thousand of nerve endings. This is why it is so sensitive to stroking.

While stroking, you can keep the finger flat on the clitoris and stroke with the full finger's length.

You can as well touch the clitoris with the top of your finger only and stroke her up and down.

It's essential as well to offer the exact right amount of pressure.

Start with extreme gentleness! As if you were touching a feather.

While you stroke, ask her if she enjoys more pressure or simply try a tiny bit more yourself and see how she responds.

When you experiment with this clitoris massage practice, you might be surprised to realize how much pressure some women can take.

If you can, get her to be totally physically still so that you can concentrate on her without losing contact with her clitoris.

Many women say that they simply prefer the gentle touch of a wet finger on their clitoris.

That's what makes them cum the fastest.

Take your time by the way. This is not a race or a competition.

Compliment her on the beauty of the texture of her inner and outer lips.

Let her know that you enjoy what you see.

If she orgasms, her clitoris can become extremely sensitive and she might reject your touch.

No worries, this extreme sensitivity moment usually lasts only for a minute and if she is open for it, you can head for a multiple orgasm session.

How much clitoris or vaginal stimulation she needs is different for every woman.

Ask her and explore it together. Listen to what she says and be open to change what you had in mind.

Listen! She will give you essential clues about what she likes or not.

Rather than a finger, you can of course use your tongue for clitoris stimulation.

Try different moves and see what she responds to the best.

Play with different pressures, your lips, various angles.

You can for instance use your full flat tongue on her vaginal and clitoris area.

You can as well play only with the tip of your tongue and focus more exclusively on her clitoris.

Again, use a finger to slide the hood that covers her clitoris, so that the tip of your tongue really is in direct contact with her clitoris.

Another technique is to slightly bite the clit area between your lips.

Be careful not to touch her with your teeth though! Use ONLY your lips.

Now, Go and explore!

Practice! This is what makes you good at it.

Clitoris stimulation represents only one aspect of yoni massage.

In this article I talk about the woman having orgasms but in so many of the tantric sex practices it is actually more productive not to bring her all the way to orgasm.

Erotic Power!

Do you need intercourse to create sexual union?

You don't need to have sex to share sexual energies with someone.

There can be dozens of reasons why you might not want to have sex with your partner.

Dozens of techniques can stimulate the exchange of energy between your two bodies and create this intense sense of unity and love between the two of you.

You have as well various levels of intimacy you can engage into.

For instance you might be comfortable with nakedness.

You might take it one step further with kisses and light intimacy.

You might even stimulate each other sexually.

Or take it all the way to sexual intercourse.

All these various intimacy stages are worlds in themselves.

You can wear clothes and only engage into synchronized dynamic breathing techniques for instance.

With this practice only, you can already incredibly expand the energy exchange between your two beings.

It works and it is limitless! REALLY!

A simple technique can take you a very long way.

You can practice it once and it can already feel like a big smile of energy in you.

You can as well, take that specific technique and practice it every day for a few minutes for instance.

I like this open approach where you feel free to engage in erotic energy exchanges according exactly to what you want or what you feel comfortable with.

Maybe you will take a small step and within a few days, know that you want to explore more intimate techniques.

Again, all doors and directions are open.

If you don't know what direction to take, I can certainly help you find what fits you best.

Remember that all this is free and open.

You can reinvent sex according to your own needs and desires. Once you start practicing these techniques, you own them and develop them in your own unique way.

Shouldn't we suppress desire?

This question is essential and it is one that many people struggle with.

What is the best attitude towards sex?

Is it better to put a lid on it?

Or is it better to use it and master it, creating beauty and love?

Again, you are free to choose what suits you best.

You have so many different approaches because different people have different needs.

Sex is beautiful! If it wasn't for it, there would be no life on this planet.

How could the act which creates life be condemned?

Again, this is only one opinion and you are totally free to disagree with this statement.

If you struggle with your sexual energy and trying to suppress sex didn't work too well, then erotic exploration is definitely an option for you.

In my own experience, embracing and using your sexual energy rather than trying to put a lid on it is a very powerful transformation tool.

Again, you are free and you have many possible ways to go.

Sexual exploration is only one of them.

Desire is beautiful!

Remove shame or guilt!

Somehow, society has developed this attitude or energy towards sexual desire, sexual exchange.

It feels like sexual desire for someone is something that people should be ashamed of.

Why?

Why did it come to that?

Take this example:

Suppose you are a man.

You go to a party.

You start chatting with this girl.

You start feeling aroused by her presence.

You start having fantasies about having sex with her right there.

Now, would you tell her?

Of course not, right?

The question is: WHY?

WHY NOT?

Is it "inappropriate"?

Is it insulting?

Do you diminish her in any way by feeling sexual desire towards her?

Something is happening in your mind and body right there.

This thing is sexual desire.

It is because of sexual desire that people have sex, procreate and each one of us is alive on this planet because of it!

We should be thankful for sexual desire and celebrate each time we feel it!

Really!

It is a delicious emotion that brings sparks of energy in people's lives.

Where did the shame come from?

Who defines what's appropriate or not?

Why would sex be something dirty that needs to be hidden?

Do you realize how much these beliefs shape society and human interactions?

In the example I mentioned above, what you really say when you express your desire to have sex with her is:

"I find you incredibly attractive and while I enjoy this conversation with you, I feel like touching your hair and kissing your lips.

I want to remove your clothes, be naked together and engage in a sexual dance with you. I am filled with desire to have you in my arms..."

See?

Beautiful, right?

You just gave her a whole set of delicious compliments.

You told her that you like her, appreciate her beauty and are profoundly touched by her presence.

You feel a connection and want to express that connection.

By the way, if you are a woman feeling sexual desire for a man, the same applies. Same if you are gay as well.

That's what I see.

Sexual desire is a gift!

Feeling it is a blessing!

How to reach sexual bliss

When you reach sexual bliss the idea of orgasm is totally gone.

This "explosive" orgasmic experience is transmuted into a continuous state of bliss which can last for hours, days or even longer.

If you are very experienced with erotic play, you might even enter into a permanent state of bliss.

At that stage, even the need for sex can disappear.

This is the moment when your sexual desire and energy fully bursts into the other chakras and creates a whole new state of consciousness and awareness.

It can take long to fully master these states of bliss.

Mastering them means being able to create them and intensify them at will.

Again, the most important element is that sex is no longer used as a mean for procreation or short term orgasmic gratification.

It is consciously used as a source of infinite energy.

The inner transformations associated with erotic play take some harmonizing time to integrate.

The idea is to practice yoga, exercise and eat healthy at the same time.

These side practices allow you to integrate these new energies much faster and harmonize them within your being.

Sexual mastery for women

Do you want to be in love?

Of course you do!

You like the feeling of having a crush too!

Now, what is VERY alienating is when you have a crush and no way of fulfilling your desires.

That's when it hurts!

It's stressful and creates pain!

You don't want to get rid of the sexual attraction, the desire, the lust, the sex!

All these are perfect!

They are energy and they make you feel alive.

What is not nice is to feel alienated or enslaved by emotions you have no idea how to tame, direct or control.

That's the place that really hurts.

Ultimately, it is about mastering your sexual energy and being to play with it at will.

You want as well to generate sexual connection with any person you want.

That's the dream of every woman, of every girl.

It is to be able to get in a guy's head and get him to like you back.

Here is the thing: I believe it is actually possible.

I see women expressing qualities that make them super attractive to men all the time.

Some of it has to do with looks of course, character, ambitions, sexiness, flirting skills, etc.

These are the usual things but there is one more that I think is the key!

This one is usually not expressed or described or talked about enough!

It is SEXUAL CONFIDENCE.

More than that! It is about being able to fulfill and man's profound sexual desires.

The key is energy sex.

What does that mean?

That you know how to trigger and stimulate a man's desire.

You can trigger it through your attitude, the way you touch him, the way you stimulate him sexually.

That's when you REALLY hit the holly grail of sexual attraction and get in a man's mind.

You need to be able to stimulate a man's energy at will and truly own this skill.

To tell you the truth sexual intercourse is only a small fraction of these skills.

You have to put yourself in the position of the one who wants to serve this man as Shiva!

You see him like a God and you are a Goddess.

Don't worry, this is a 2 ways things and the situation will be reversed.

This means men will worship you as well and fulfill your deepest desires.

But for now, let's focus first on what you can give a man that will get him to come back to you over and over again for more.

You see, in most cases, men and women will have sex, one or both of them orgasms and this is it.

If the man loses semen, he will usually fall in the after sex stage.

This means that his sexual desire drops and his level of attraction towards you can collapse as well.

Even if you share a romantic moment afterwards by holding each other for instance, the following day, his desire to have sex with you could be much lower.

So, the key is to get him to hold his semen for much longer and even not lose it at all.

Put it this way: who will want to see you more the following day? A guy who is still burning with desire for you or the one who has already lost semen and is in the after sex stage?

You know that, right?

A man ejaculating before your orgasm can be one of the most frustrating sexual experiences you can have.

It changes everything!

You see him drifting away in a TOTALLY different reality.

You feel suddenly an emotional gap appearing between the two of you.

The reason this gap exists is because the energy that was fueling the emotional connection is gone.

It is really that simple!

A huge part of romantic love has to do with sexual attraction!

This is how we were programmed by nature: to procreate.

So much of our social interactions and the way we handle them is about managing and triggering sexual desire.

So, back to men feeling attracted to you...

The moment you give a man incredible pleasure and are super confident with your sexual skills, guys come back to you over and over again.

Do you realize that some men will pay $300-$1000 just to experience that with an erotic goddess?

Erotic goddess is a nice way of saying "sacred courtesan" or "sacred prostitute".

We are talking about skills, sexual skills.

You can be a erotic master and express your skills with just one man you feel committed to.

Or you can have an uncommitted approach and have sex with many partners.

All these are variations and you need to find for yourself what suits you.

My point is that whatever way you want to express them, what you want are sexual confidence or sexual mastery.

These are skills!

They are your ability to tame Eros, desire and sexual energy in a man's body and stimulate them at will.

When you lay on a massage table and you have a skilled massage therapist taking care of you, how does that make you feel?

A very skilled massage therapist can even take you to a mystical state and literally open a consciousness gateway in you.

That's skilled touch and that's the exact type of skill you need to develop if you want to connect with any man you want and get them to be and stay attracted to you.

That's the dance of Eros.

It is the art of mastering sexual energy in you and in others.

Guys can actually get bored with sex.

If what they experience with you is not exciting enough they will go and look somewhere else.

So, if you have everything, character, energy, beauty and feel that you still don't click with men you are attracted to, these are the skills you want to develop.

Practically, what are we talking about?

It is a infinite set of possibilities.

We are not talking about just a simple trick, ok?

We are talking about embodying EXACTLY what any man profoundly wants!

What they want is YOU TO BE ABLE TO BRING THEM TO A STATE OF ABSOLUTE, TOTAL MYSTICAL TRANCE THROUGH THE ACTIVATION AND MASTERY OF THEIR SEXUAL ENERGY.

Again, it's a two ways thing!

So yes! A skilled male Daka or Tantrika will do this for you too.

Once you know that this is in fact what you want to develop, finding the techniques and practicing them is actually easy.

That's not the challenge.

The real challenge is to align yourself with that energy.

That's were many women fail because they don't know how to connect with that stream.

These skills we talk about are part of an inner school, an inner teaching which has been on the planet for a long time.

Over the centuries, these skills reappear here and there through the impulse of some erotic master.

Manifested erotic schools do exist but you can access these skills internally as well.

You can develop them.

These skills don't BELONG to just one tradition. They go beyond borders and limits.

They are free and open all over the world.

All you need is a desire to explore them and they will come to you.

The key words here are:

SEXUAL CONFIDENCE.

SEXUAL MASTERY.

MASTERY OF SEXUAL ENERGIES.

When you develop these qualities, it gives you a whole new edge in the way you relate to men!

And believe me; I have seen quite a few women express these skills!

It's unbelievable to see the desire they trigger in men instantly.

Don't be mistaken, ok? This is very far away from the porn stream.

What we talk about here is NOT some superficial experience based on a commercial system.

It is not cheap, slutty or vulgar.

We are talking about something that goes way deeper than that.

It is refined! It is an art!

It is a spiritual stream that opens energy gateways in your body and mind.

And yes! That's any man's most profound desire!

This is what gives you the final dating or sex edge that guys are really looking for.

When you have it and embody it, you have it for life!

It's a set of skills, attitudes and a incredible level of sexual confidence that you will NEVER forget!

THIS is what you are looking for.

You can go around in circles testing everything I said.

You can look for alternatives and other ways to access a man's mind.

You will eventually come back to what I am saying now.

Many women realize this when they are in their 40's or 50's after a broken marriage or a series of frustrating relationships.

Every single woman I know is in fact looking for these skills.

The ones who already have them want to perfect them.

Every love and desire you ever had in your existence can be fulfilled once you master sexual energy in you and in men.

Mastering doesn't mean control, ok?

It means playing with it at will!

Being able to stimulate it or silent it at will.

His Shakti quest

Shakti is life force.

It is a universal principle.

Very often Shakti is used in a more specific way to define feminine qualities.

It is in that way I use it in this article...

Shakti is what a man looks for when he engages in connecting with a woman.

When he wants to experience her femininity, what he really wants to feel is this femininity inside of him.

He wants to merge with her mind so that the Shakti she gives you is a direct inner experience in you.

When he makes love, he wants to experience the play of energies IN him.

The sensations triggers are chain of biochemical reactions in his brain and body.

These are happening right in his being.

Within the tantric tradition, Shakti is life force!

She is a Goddess!

She is the consort of Shiva.

A woman will be a messenger for Shakti so that a man can experience this energy in him.

Shakti triggers pleasure, delight, beauty, harmony and freedom!

When he touches her skin, when he feels aroused by her presence, it is because her Shakti force impacts on his being.

He feels an opening!

He feels a streaming of new energy inside of him.

Now, this Shakti force is an experience a man can have in many other contexts, not just erotic exchange with a woman.

He can experience Shakti through artistic expression, singing and music, being in nature or invoking the Shakti force in him through meditation.

In fact, most of the tantric path - the full tantric path, not just tantric sex - is aimed at mastering Shakti.

It is aimed at fully understanding how to play with this energy and how to transmit it too.

Imagine for instance that you are in nature with a music instrument and that you are touched by the beauty of the landscape.

You play some music that expresses this beauty.

You create a piece that you play later for your friends.

By listening to this music, your friends experience the beauty you felt.

That's one example of mastering this Shakti energy.

You had an experience which was the merging of your energy with nature.

Then, you take that experience and turn this Shakti force into a refined musical piece that you use to initiate others into that experience.

In Sanskrit, nature is Prakriti!

It is essence and is simply another name for Shakti.

So... When a man experiences Shakti through erotic connection with a woman, this woman is his agent and initiates a stream of Shakti energy in him.

When a man is in love with that woman, he is in fact in love with that experience!

He is in love with the experience of Shakti because Shakti freed his sexual energy and mind.

This is simply a way of describing something which is of course much deeper.

A man is to be able to master Shakti with or without a woman.

When he feels extremely needy sexually, it means that he feels desperations.

He gets the impression that if a woman doesn't trigger this Shakti experience in him, he will have no way of accessing it by himself.

This isn't true!

Accessing his own Shakti power is a skill he can develop.

In fact, I believe this is one of the core challenges men face in life.

When he discovers how to master and activate his own Shakti flow, he enters into a whole new dimension in life.

That's a new state of unity and bliss!

He feels united with the world around him and joy streams through his being.

He is one!

He has many possible pathways to master his own Shakti energy.

My favorites are music, singing, dancing, sensual exchange with a woman, swimming in the clear waters of a lake or a river and so many more.

Both men and women can use these approaches to tap in their Shakti power.

Another VERY direct way to connect with Shakti and invite her in your life is to use the Sanskrit mantra for Shakti:

If you simply write this mantra frequently, you will start building the connection with this Shakti power inside of you.

You will create space to start playing with this Shakti force + You will as well be inspired to create more forms associated with Shakti.

These techniques are for both men and women.

For instance, some women will have very little connection with their Shakti power and could develop it way deeper.

Some men will have total mastery over their Shakti force and need to connect with their male power or Shiva power instead.

If you are in a gay relationship, roles might be redefined too.

And even for a woman who fully expresses her Shakti power, sex play with a strong male might trigger even further the flow of her Shakti force.

It might empower her even further in her femininity.

So, this is NOT just a simple model.

These are general ideas and as with any romantic vision, this description is only a simplified picture of a reality which is way more complex.

Take what you can, use it and reshape it in your own way!

Depending on the way you look at it, you can see Shakti in every aspect of human life.

There is Shakti in business, in science and politics not just in arts!

Shakti is EVERYWHERE because it is a universal principle permeating all aspects of life on this planet.

The opposite is true as well.

In many cases, the refined channels of creative art and beauty can be locked or limited within lines of expression which are very rational and in which the Shakti flow is not present.

For instance, when you wake up in the morning, your intention is very often to deal with very practical things.

You will take a shower, make some breakfast and your whole focus might be to get to work.

The purpose of these actions is to maintain your life + get to work to express some of your creative power and make money.

Now imagine what would happen if you wipe out this whole scenario and you replace it by something totally different.

You wake up in the morning and your purpose for the day is to generate beauty and delight.

You take a shower with your partner and take time to explore the sensuality of this moment.

After that you prepare a delicious smoothie and take very special care in giving it a delicious exotic taste.

Then, you take your music instrument and let your fingers explore the inspiration of the moment while you are surrounded by picture of dancing goddesses.

In all these activities, the purpose is not money or practical.

The purpose is to manifest beauty and delicious sensations.

This is a VERY specific quest.

The Shakti we talk about here is beauty, refinement, delight and pleasure.

When you are able to manifest these qualities at will anytime you want, you can say that you mastered the Shakti energy.

You are a Shakti Master.

Tantric sex techniques

When you think of tantric sex, you might get the feeling that it's all about complicated positions.

This is very far away from the truth.

The first posture is not a physical one; it is a mental or emotional one.

The physical aspects of tantra are quite simple. In fact you don't need complicated sexual positions.

All you need is the understanding and vision of how your sexual energy will be transmuted.

Of course, it can be fun to try some complex positions.

Yes! They might add a new dimension to your tantric sex experience.

However, you can achieve all this inner growth even if you keep your tantric sex approaches very simple.

How to preserve your sexual energies

One of the key tantric sex strategies is to preserve your energies and make them grow.

When you have sex, usually the final goal is to reach an orgasm.

Forget about this picture and imagine what happens if you don't go for the orgasm.

Imagine that there is no loss of semen for the man and that all the sexual excitement build up stays within.

Now, imagine that you don't come for months and that every time you have sex, you keep on building energy and increasing your level of inner sexual tension.

As you can imagine, this might lead to some intense energy build up.

The only way to find out what happens is to try and practice it.

Now, this is probably one of the most challenging trainings you can go for in life.

Everything in your instinctual nature encourages you to let go of your semen and have an orgasm.

So, it takes focus and determination to shift this pattern and simply hold back before you reach the "no return" point.

What about women?

As a woman, you can practice the same.

You can simply come to the limit of your orgasm and then, simply keep this potential inside.

In tantric sex, we talk a lot about transmutation of energies.

The sexual energy rises through your chakras and activates them.

It eventually reaches the heart chakra and creates a whole new sexual experience.

What happens?

I guess everyone will experience this differently but generally, you will enter into an expansion of the heart area.

This means that your level of love for your partner and anything else in the universe will suddenly grow immensely.

Those who experienced it talk about a profound and transforming mystical experience.

This experience does not stop there.

The rising of sexual energies can expand into the third eye and crown chakra as well and create this immense sense of clarity and understanding.

All these experiences are mystical or spiritual experiences.

You can experience them through meditation or other practices.

In that case, you use sexual union and awakening as the vehicle to manifest these blissful states.

So, you have two directions you can go:

- **The first one is to approach sex the traditional way**. You have sex. You orgasm or ejaculate. You enter into an after sex state. This means usually that the sexual tension and build up is released.

- **The second one is to practice tantric sex and energy build up**. You use sexual energy as an inner force which will create a series of mystical experiences in you.

How long does it take to reach a state of inner bliss and fulfillment with your partner?

I would say one to three months of very focused tantric sex practice.

If you are already familiar with these techniques and have been meditating a lot before, these experiences might appear much faster.

Does it mean that you need to have sex 10 hours a day for a month?

In a way, yes! But you don't need to go that far of course.

The goal is to ingrate tantric sex practices in your daily life until it becomes totally natural for you and your partner.

The next step would be to be in an ideal protected setting.

It can be a holiday place, resort, nature location or spiritual retreat situation.

In these contexts, you can use all your resources and energy to focus on this inner transformation process.

What if you can't step out of your routine and need to stay at home, work and focus on all your daily tasks?

You will of course still practice tantric sex in that context.

The benefits and experiences you will get are very intense no matter what.

It simply means that you might tend to get more distracted by other daily practicalities and will need to focus on lots of other things, not just your tantric practices.

The results are still there!

Practicing tantric sex from exactly where you are is definitely the best way to go.

In a way, there is no need to go anywhere. You can create your own tantric temple at home and design a very harmonious and healthy life style conductive for profound changes.

The tantric sex path can be practiced anywhere.

All you need is to start moving.

Sexual dreams and fantasies

This is an essential part of your erotic experience.

The buildup of sexual energy will often be associated with a fertile sexual imagination.

Your sexual energy simply feeds your mind and activates your fantasy world.

It is normal.

You might see yourself having sex with other women or men.

You might have visions or desires you did not have before.

All this is healthy and normal.

Most of these fantasies <u>are not meant to be manifested</u>.

They are simply the mind reflection of your sexual awakening.

In the beginning, some of these images can almost be shocking because you envision scenes you can feel ashamed of.

No worries again.

All this is normal and is a simple "clarification" of your mind.

Enjoy these visions and fantasies.

Don't focus too much on them as if it was something meant to happen.

Simply observe them as if you were watching a movie on a screen.

Every now and then, see if you can influence these fantasies.

Remove those you don't like and stimulate those which do thrill and excite you.

How to explore erotic play in your couple

One key is open communication.

You need to share not only on the sexual level but on the verbal level as well.

The goal is to create synergy and complicity.

You need to understand and respect the limits of your partner.

You need to listen and share.

The best way to do this is to set time aside to talk about what you experience.

Be open minded.

The next step is to protect your erotic space.

Not all times are suitable for practicing.

Sometimes, your partner won't be in the mood or simply too tired.

Respect is truly the key word for your couple.

Don't ever push or force. You will generate the exact opposite result to what you expected if you do.

One of the key challenges for modern couples is to find space and time for intimacy.

When you are rushing the whole week with practicalities it can be very challenging to find a romantic moment for you and your partner.

Focus on it and start creating time.

Find out if erotic play is an exploration you both want to invest into.

Again, dialogue, respect and love are the key values you must remember at all times

Solo erotic play - Path of self pleasure

The path of self pleasure means that you explore erotic play by yourself.

This offers you a space to train your erotic skills, experience your limits and understand how pleasure manifests in your body.

Because you are by yourself, it offers you the perfect setting to explore an aspect of your sexuality in depth.

We talked earlier about delicious experiences arising as a result of erotic play, right?

In a way, you can achieve the same type of results through solo tantric sex.

You can wake up your sexual energy to the point of feeling it opening your heart area and the other upper chakras.

Even with solo erotic play, you are never alone.

The tantric energy which sponsors your experiences is still there of course.

See it an intelligent angelic or spiritual force activating these energies in you.

The world of your fantasies is there as well of course.

In esoteric terms, this world of fantasies is the astral reality. It is the world of emotions, dreams and desires.

You can meet people on the astral. You can actually have sex on the astral.

You can feel a person's presence without this person ever being there physically.

In a way, this solo erotic exploration gives you lots of space and freedom.

You notice that when you have tantric sex with a partner, you need to sometimes process emotions, digest, be careful with what you say or do.

This can be quite demanding in some cases.

Solo erotic play has the advantage of giving you space and freedom, which are essential to explore this path.

Another way of using solo tantric sex is simply as a form of training.

Suppose that you are a man and you want to train your lingam in order to preserve your energy.

When you are with a girl, you might get too excited to actually dive into training that skill.

Solo tantric sex will give you the ideal setting to explore this avenue without risk.

Energy orgasms

For men, energy orgasms or full body orgasms are powerful explosions of energy without the loss of semen.

For women, they are profound orgasmic experiences that touch deeper layers of the body and mind.

Because of their depth, energy orgasms can be much more fulfilling than traditional orgasms.

They are especially important for men because they allow them to have an orgasmic experience without the loss semen and therefore without much loss of energy either.

An energy dip still happens after the orgasm but this dip much smaller than if ejaculation occurs.

When you explore erotic play, energy orgasms are a good first stage to head for.

They allow you to train your tantric skills and build up your sexual energy without fully containing it.

It is essential to realize though that it's only an intermediary stage.

After a while, you will notice that even energy orgasms are no longer needed.

You can reach much higher states of maintained pleasure by fully and totally holding your energy.

Erotic play for couples

This is one of the greatest benefits of erotic practices: they strengthen your couple!

Erotic play is a binding force.

It creates a unifying fire which brings a new quality of love and refinement into your couple's life.

It can take 1 to 3 months to shift a situation which looks sexually desperate for two partners.

We are not talking about therapy here.

This is simply the awakening of a source of fire which is infinite and acts like a binding force in a relationship.

This is one of the key erotic play gold mines.

This is a new sexual expression which fits a modern need.

If you are a couple, you tend to focus a lot on life's practicalities.

It is not always easy to reconnect with your sexual drive, desire or passion.

This is where the sexual energy comes in.

Imagine connecting with a force which reawakens these qualities in you and your partner.

Imagine that your sex life suddenly wakes up from its sleep.

Imagine this romantic dimension suddenly appearing again in the core of your being.

This is exactly what erotic play can do for you.

It goes far beyond sex of course.

Sexual energy is a fire which stimulates every aspect of your relationship.

It wakes up delightful feelings and bliss naturally because these qualities are the essence of sexual energy.

Imagine having an infinite source of fire and power in you.

This is your sexual energy.

When you give it a channel of expression, it naturally flows and frees fresh energy in your being.

Start with simple steps

This is the way to go.

No need for profound revolutions.

- Get some sensual massage oils
- Add candles and incense
- Prepare a special meal and offer to eat it naked
- Etc.

There are dozens of steps you can take which will increase sensuality between the two of you.

The idea is to increase sensuality so that your sexual experience is deeper and more pleasurable on many levels.

This widens the potential of your erotic exploration.

Start by applying the simple techniques described in this book.

The goal is simple: reconquer your sexual territory.

If you want to put romance, love and passion back in the center of your life, you need a sponsoring force to help you do so.

This is what erotic play does.

It is a fire which supports these sacred qualities in your being.

As soon as you start expressing this stream in your life and connect with simple erotic play techniques, you wake up the qualities of love and passion.

Focus on manifesting and mastering this stream fully within a period of 3 months.

It does not happen overnight.

You simply reconquer your sexual and romantic territory by clearing the relationship space with this inner fire.

The results are amazing.

It takes a very short period of time to renew your sexual space and bring a total sense of freshness between you and your partner.

What if you and your partner disagree on your erotic experience?

It happens of course.

You feel like you don't have time to focus on it right now and your partner is full of burning desire for instance.

What do you do?

How do you solve differences?

It is very simple: dialogue, respect and freedom.

Tantra is a passionate fire.

It is a fire you must learn to tame.

The fact that you feel very inspired to share sex at a given moment does not mean that it <u>must</u> happen.

You can dialogue with the erotic spirit.

You can play with the erotic forces and tame them as well.

You can stimulate them or excite them when you want to and give them some rest if you feel the timing is not right.

What matters is that you are the designer of your erotic experience.

Erotic play is not a set of forms which are imposed on you by force.

It's actually the total opposite.

You have total freedom to design your erotic experience is whatever way you want.

And so does your erotic partner.

What if your partner does something that you don't like

If anything happens during the session that you don't like or doesn't work for you, don't let it build up negativity or resentment.

If it hurts or feels really uncomfortable, you can give your partner a sign that it's not really working for you.

If you can and as much as possible, try to keep that type of information for the feedback minute after the session. That way you won't interrupt each other's flow and inspired ideas.

In the feedback minute be gentle but do share what works and what doesn't.

If you get some "negative" feedback, see it as an opportunity to learn and discover new skills.

That's one of the key to mastering erotic play:

It is to accept the fact that there is a learning curve.

Your partner's feedback is essential to you as it will help you master your erotic techniques.

Also, do give feedback, both positive and negative if any.

Many people will touch you, kiss you or take some action that can feel uncomfortable, painful or be a massive turn off.

Unless you tell them, it is challenging for them to find out.

I have frequently seen and experienced both men and women taking some sexual action that they thought was arousing when in fact it's a turn off or even painful.

Remember as well that different people have different tastes too!

Something that worked with a previous erotic partner might be inappropriate or a turn off for someone else.

This is why these feedback minutes after session are so essential to keep perfecting your techniques.

How to tell your partner to increase or decrease stimulation intensity

This one is essential especially for men.

If you are a man and your female partner has no clear idea of how excited you are, she might go one step too far and make you lose semen.

That's the last thing you want!

You want to give her hints to tell her she can intensify or slow down.

The simplest way to do is to use 3 words:

- Stronger
- Softer
- Perfect

Simple, right? ;)

Another way to go is to quantify your degree of excitement. That's even more precise and works really well.

Suppose that 0% is non excited and 100% is max excitement. 100% is when you would come.

With erotic play, the goal is to navigate in the 80-90% zone without going all the way to 100% excitement.

So, you can give her hints.

For instance, if you feel she can go way further, you can say "60" or "70".

If she goes too far and you are about to come, simply say 95 to get her to slow down a bit.

You can as well use a hand sign like thumbs up for perfect, raise your hand up for more, or bring your hand down to get her to slow down.

You can use these feedback techniques if you are a woman as well.

Usually it is easier for a woman to control her orgasm and decide when she wants to come.

For a man it is usually very easy to get over stimulated and totally miss the energy build up target.

If you are a woman, keep an eye on your male partner.

More importantly, be aware that you don't want him to lose semen as this usually means the end of this erotic play session.

Set up a veto right with your partner so that you both feel safe

When you partner is leading, if you are asked to do something you REALLY don't want, let your partner know that this goes one step too far for you.

It's very healthy to have this "veto" right so that you feel totally secure in an erotic session.

As a general guideline, I would encourage you to use your veto right only in very rare, extreme cases.

Very often, a new erotic idea might stretch a bit your comfort zone.

However, dare to experiment.

As soon as you try, you will notice that you might actually like it a lot.

If your partner is leading, really let go of trying to direct.

SURRENDER!

PLAY THE GAME!

ACCEPT THAT YOUR PARTNER IS IN CHARGE FOR THIS SESSION!

Having this attitude will let them feel that you trust them and immensely energize your sexual play.

It will give power, trust and confidence to your couple and give you space to experiment.

Bring your partner and yourself to an erotic trance any time you want

If you are a woman, the goal is to be able to put him and yourself in an erotic trance any time you want.

That's when you enter into a whole new dimension in life.

The day I discovered these tools in my life through intense practice, it RADICALLY changed my vision of not just sex, but totally impacted in the way I perceive life and male/female interactions as well.

I honestly believe that this is EXACTLY what you look for and is easily accessible to you.

Naked dinner!

That's an exciting way to set up your erotic session.

Prepare some nice fresh raw dishes, get naked and set up your erotic space by the fire place in your living room

Or you can set up your dinner erotic play session in your bedroom or whatever place you use as your favorite space.

Eating naked with your partner is an incredibly sensual experience.

Prepare the space and your bodies with delicious scents and oils. Put on your erotic jewelry and whatever triggers your erotic energy.

You can start playing straight away while you eat which can totally multiply the pleasure you get from it.

Set it up and enjoy it!

You will be amazed by how delightful this experience can be!

What is the best time for sex?

Honestly? Any time works!

For instance you can have a whole week end focused on sex with in depth exploration of your new skills...

Or you can have a morning quick energetic session before you get up...

Or you can have a 15 min lunch sex break.

Or have a whole evening dedicated to erotic pleasure.

All of these options work! No need to limit yourself!

Now, I believe that amongst ALL these possible choices, the one that suits best our natural rhythms is evening 8-10pm.

You don't have to stretch your session for 2 hours of course. You can have for instance a 30 or 60 min erotic play session around that time of the evening.

If you want to develop your sex skills, I believe that's the best time to practice.

A 2 hours space gives you plenty of time to dive into it.

The evening creates a refined and romantic energy.

Lower the lights, uses candles and incense.

You can really set it up like a daily erotic play meeting with your partner.

Stronger - Softer - Perfect

These 3 words are 3 core feedback indicators you can use in erotic play to tell your partner what you need.

You don't need to use them all the time of course.

Very often, it's way more exciting to let your partner search for the absolute best way to please you without saying a word...

How long should an erotic session last?

It depends of course on the circumstances.

Week days might need shorter sessions whereas weekends give you more space.

If you are new to active erotic exploration, I would definitely start with short 15 min sessions max.

They can even be shorter to 5 or 10 min.

Check with your partner and make sure you agree on a time frame.

It's important that you check if you or your partner has to leave soon or if you have plenty of time.

In my opinion, having frequent short sessions works slightly better than one long 2 hours session once a week for instance.

Think of the way you eat for instance. You have a meal or snack every 3 hours, right?

Or when you train your body, you build up your level of fitness by exercising every day for an hour rather than just running a marathon on Sunday, right?

Erotic play is an energy you build following the same type of principles.

You can build up sexual energy in the same way, by having short tantric sex moments throughout the day or the week.

Of course, a one time long practice in the week end is totally an option too and will work perfectly if that's what you prefer.

It's essential to always check with your partner to see the time that suits you both best.

Is it day time during the week, week days evenings, evenings in weekends, middle of the night when you feel a desire rush?

Timing is super important and identifying what works best for your couple will strongly empower your erotic practices.

Once you are comfortable with short sessions, you can extend these sessions to 30 min and eventually 1 hour or a few hours.

It could easily take you a couple of months to build up your energy to the point where you can easily go for a 2 hours erotic session.

Remember though that you want to leave on a high with the feeling that you could easily go on if you wanted to.

Many people who start with active erotic play will make the mistake of wanting to press all the juice out of a session.

They experience a bit of this delicious bliss and don't want to let it go by fear of not being able to recreate that experience again.

Remember that the goal is to be able to play with your sexual energy at will.

You can trigger it any time you want and even play with its intensity.

That's one of the core targets of tantric sex.

To your sexual power!

How to start and finish an erotic session

One good way to go is simply to sit in front of each other cross legged and have a short meditation minute.

You can do this with open or closed eyes.

Synchronize your breathing.

Smile!

This gives you the possibility to refocus your energy and create space in your mind.

Join your hands in front of your heart or third eye chakra in a prayer position.

You can as well express your wishes for this session internally or verbally to your partner.

You can say for instance: "I want to invoke the erotic spirit and infinite love - I want to give my partner immense pleasure and bring him (or her) to absolute bliss - I want our energies to merge and be one..."

This is of course just an example.

You can spontaneously say your own invocation.

You can as well ask for guidance or help.

Again, this can be done internally or out loud.

You can speak in your own name or in the name of your couple.

Erotic minute

Along the same line as having a 15 tantric energy boost, you can do this for just a minute.

It can be in the form of an energy technique you practice together, a kissing minute, a quick lingam or yoni stimulation.

You can as well have sex with intercourse for just a minute.

Waking up desire this way without consuming it for more than a minute can leave you with a high degree of excitement for the evening for instance.

You can as well practice this consciously and if circumstances allow it, have for instance 20 erotic energy minutes spread during the day.

You can decide to meet every 30 min for instance at fixed times.

Or you can go to your partner and play with them for a just a minute.

For this practice, it's important that you drop it after a minute. You trigger the excitement and desire for a minute and let go.

You can practice this at fixed times every 30 min or you can keep it open and spontaneously go to your partner when you want, at random intervals and play for an erotic minute.

In this erotic minute, you can practice an energy technique, yoni or lingam kissing, yoni or lingam massage, kissing, any form of sensual touch and even intercourse.

Tantric sex - Energy breaks

You don't need a whole hour or lots of time to engage in tantric sex play.

A 15 min quick tantric energy impulse can do wonders.

You can have various levels of intimacy when engaging in such energy exchange.

You can as well boost your day by having frequent breaks like this one spread during the day.

Your desire stays then high for hours afterwards triggering exciting fantasies and the desire to meet again later.

Try it!

Different people might have different tastes

Something that worked with a previous tantric sex partner might not necessarily work for someone else.

Your new partner might find it inappropriate, uncomfortable or even be turned off by it.

Here are some examples of these possible differences from person to person:

- How much pressure she likes on her clitoris.

- Type of favorite stimulation, finger, tongue or intercourse.

- Favorite sex position.

- Being turned on or turned off when you see your partner pleasuring themselves.

- Openness to invite other people to play with your couple.

- The best time for sex.

- How much structure to give to your tantric sex session.

- Being totally passive while your partner stimulates you.

- Etc.

When you check it, you see that there many variations from person to person.

It is always good to ask your partner to get a confirmation.

The simplest questions to ask are:

- How does that feel?
- Do you like it when I do that?
- From these two options which one do you prefer?
- Etc.

Plan your erotic play sessions

You have two ways to go with tantric sex sessions.

The first one is to follow your passion and simply engage with your partner spontaneously when you feel like it.

The second one is to plan your sessions.

Both approaches work really well, so you can experiment and see what suits you best.

Why plan?

Because everyone is very busy these days and if you want to consciously engage in a tantric energy build up, planning your session will secure that space and prioritize this activity.

The best times for sessions are morning after waking up and especially evenings when energy enters in the refinement mode.

Decide who will be leading, that way the one who leads can choose one or more techniques, the length for the session and prepare the space.

I know that planning a tantric sex session can feel less passionate, romantic or spontaneous but it is VERY powerful.

To get turned on and wake up desire, you can initiate practice with some dynamic breathing techniques, yoga poses, an energy building technique or a kissing minute.

Even if you are not into it at first, your desire can wake up very fast. Once you give each other's bodies a bit of attention you are usually ready to go!

We plan yoga sessions, training at the gym and all sorts of other activities. Why not plan your tantric sex sessions?

If you rely on simply finding spare time for tantric sex after long and busy days, you might systematically end up with late night practices or even be too tired to even engage into it.

When you plan it and consciously open space for it, you empower your tantric sex life immensely.

You give it time and give it priority too!

Interval stimulation - Build up energy and avoid over excitement

This one is especially useful to avoid over stimulation and loss of semen.

It allows you as well to build up tantric energy for much longer so that sessions last for one or even a few hours.

This technique is simple.

Suppose that you are a woman and that you stimulate your partner's lingam with a strong hold massage technique.

He is lying on his back and you are sitting cross legged on his side next to him.

Here is what you do:

Instead of stimulating him continuously for minutes, you follow the rhythm of your conscious breathing technique.

Choose a breathing technique.

It can be any breathing sequence.

Synchronize this breathing technique with your partner so that you two follow the exact same rhythm.

The simplest approach is to breath in for 8 sec, hold for 16 sec, breath out for 8 sec.

You stimulate your male partner's lingam only when you hold your breath.

On the breathe in and breathe out, you stop massaging him but keep your hand on his lingam if he can take it.

Remember that you and your partner synchronize your breathing.

This means again that he will be stimulated only when he is holding his breath.

It builds up excitement and erotic energy without taking the risk of losing semen.

Because you consciously regulate how much stimulation you apply to his lingam, you can literally last for hours with that one.

In the beginning, start with 5 min, have a feedback minute with your partner.

Once you are ready with first tests, you can progressively increase the session's length to 15 min, 30 min, 1 hour and even 2 or more hours.

To ad variation, you can change positions and for instance he can kneel or stand. You have many possible positions for lingam stimulation and I will describe them in detail in another post.

Of course, as with other techniques, you can reverse the roles and have your partner massage your yoni using the exact same rhythm.

You can as well use this technique as a self pleasure approach when your partner's not around.

That's a super powerful technique to build up tantric energy and get sessions to last way longer.

Synchronize your breathing

At any moment of your tantric exchange you can use this simple breathing synchronization.

Simply take a minute or more to breath at the same time following the same rhythm.

That's a powerful to get in tune with each other and connect.

Combine a breathing technique with sexual stimulation

Use a breathing technique with sexual stimulation.

For instance if you are a man and your tantric partner massages your lingam, you can practice for instance the following technique:

- Breathe in for 8 sec
- Hold for 8 sec
- Breathe out for 8 sec

Take deep breaths as you practice this.

If you get too excited, you can ask your partner to massage you more softly so that she doesn't over stimulate you.

Another way to go is to let her stimulate you only when you hold your breath.

This means that she stops massaging you when you breathe in and breathe out.

Once you get used to this technique, you can stretch the "hold" time to 16 sec for instance.

You simply count internally.

Why is this such a powerful technique?

Because the alternation of rest and stimulation combined with this conscious breathing technique builds up an incredible amount of energy and sexual flow in you.

You can practice this technique for just 5 min in the beginning.

Once you and your partner get used to it, you can stretch the time to 15 min and eventually to even longer 30 or 60 min sessions.

There is no limit.

You can of course use lingam kissing stimulation instead of hand if you like.

You can as well reverse the roles and stimulate her yoni using the same type of rhythm.

This is just a first hint:

The core idea is always the same no matter which way you go. In this case it is to combine sexual stimulation with a breathing technique.

You have dozens of other possible techniques that you can use.

This is a vast topic in the yoga field.

That's a first hint.

It's incredibly powerful to build up tantric energy!

Set a time length for the session before you start

Timing is super important.

Your partner might have to leave soon, need rest or have the whole afternoon to play.

You don't know, right?

Find out BEFORE you start playing!

That way, you are warned and you both know for how long this session will go.

Imagine that you are in the middle of a super intense tantric wave and your partner tells you they have to leave.

If you don't know about it, it can hit you and not feel nice at all.

For how long should your erotic session last?

If you are new with it, start with short 5-15 min sessions.

Once you gain practice and are in tune with each other, you can stretch these sessions for 1 to a few hours.

Make sure that you check with each other before you start and decide for how long you want to practice.

This will avoid interrupting each other's flow without warning.

Of course if you know you have the full night for each other, you can be way more flexible and go with passion's flow.

Less structure and more spontaneity is super exciting too.

Keep the communication channels open with your partner and make sure that you both agree and like whatever you decide.

Tantric sex + Yoga poses

Combining tantric sex with yoga poses is incredibly arousing.

It could be because when you take a pose, you already activate your life force.

Adding sexual stimulation can take these poses to a whole new dimension of pure pleasure.

What does it look like?

Here is an example:

If your partner is a male, taking the poses and you are a female, you can for instance kiss his lingam with every pose. I don't mean just a gentle kiss on the surface. I mean actively stimulating him with your tongue and lips.

As he holds each posture, find the best way to reach his lingam and kiss them with delight.

Play with this! It's really lots of fun.

Let him hold the pose for a bit longer than he would if he was alone.

Then let him shift pose and join him again by approaching your lips to his lingam.

You can use your hands, whole body or just tongue and lips.

For instance, only using tongue and lips will create lots of excitement as it brings this extra desire call which stays suspended.

You can flow like that between a few poses and literally have a whole yoga session in which you simply ad this lingam stimulation with your lips and tongue.

This means that the session can go on from a few minutes, a few poses to an hour or more if you like.

If you are new with it, start with short sessions like 5-15 min.

Once you gain practice and are in tune with each other, you can stretch these sessions for longer.

Make sure you check with each other before you start and decide for how long you want to practice.

This will avoid interrupting each other's flow without warning.

While he takes the poses, you can as well shift practice and instead of kissing his lingam, get him to kiss your yoni.

Here is how you can do this:

You can let him take the pose and ask him to stretch his tongue out. Then, gently approach your yoni and feel his tongue massaging you or even penetrating you.

As his hands might be busy and because it could be even more arousing, you can again avoid touch with any other part of the body.

This means that only his tongue and lips can touch you.

If you want stronger stimulation, press your yoni slightly harder or closer to his lips so that he can kiss you with his full flat tongue and lips.

To hold the position, you can as well gently hold his head in the right direction. This allows him to increase his kissing pressure on your yoni.

You can of course alternate roles and if you were the female kissing his lingam, you can now for instance take the poses and let him kiss your yoni too.

You can as well let him penetrate you with every pose you take. Find the right position and get him to slide his lingam in you. You can hold the poses for a few seconds with or without movement, let him withdraw and take a new pose.

You can as well engage in more full body massage practices while posing, using lots of oils and giving special attention to lingam and yoni!

Wild, right? Are you turned on yet?

Of course, all variations of this tantric sex play are possible.

Use your imagination and take it as a practice you can develop and dive into.

As you can see, there is some structure to it.

It is not just a wild and spontaneous sex exchange.

Adding this type of VERY SUBTLE structure to a tantric sex session gives you the space to expand your horizons consciously and explore new forms of pleasure you might not find otherwise.

Alternate between you and your partner to lead tantric sex sessions

You can alternate the leading role in a session or between sessions.

The easiest way to go is to decide before the session who will be leading and let that person lead for a whole tantric session.

Another exciting way to go is to alternate leading role during the session.

For instance you can lead for 10 min and then let your partner lead for another 10 min.

Or you can bring in an idea, practice it and let your partner bring in the next idea.

If one of you is way more inspired, has many wishes and the other is comfortable with being led, one partner can keep the leadership role for a few sessions or even all the time IF IT'S SOMETHING YOU BOTH want.

I would say that in most situations, alternating the leadership role is more balanced and gives space and power to each one of you.

Remember that these "technicalities" are something you discuss together before or after a tantric sex session.

Choose who will be leading before the tantric session

A simple way to choose what to do in a tantric session is to decide who will be leading the session before you start.

Why is it important?

Because you and your partner might have different ideas and fantasies about what you want to share.

To avoid conflict, discussions or having to make choices, simply choose who the leader is for that session.

Accept the fact that you can experiment of course. It is ok to take some small risks and expand your sexual horizon.

Keep an eye on your partner.

Ask questions like "Does this feel good?", "Do you prefer this or that?" etc.

Don't engage though in a rational discussion while in the tantric sex session as this totally kills the excitement and the tantric flow. Keep that for the feedback minute after your session or in the following hours or days afterwards.

If you are leading, trust yourself and make choices, take decisions! This will give rhythm to your tantric play.

You can lead, verbally or with body language, guiding your partner with your hands.

If you are asked to do something you REALLY don't want to do, let your partner know that this goes one step too far for you.

It's very healthy to have this "veto" right so that you feel totally secure in a tantric session.

As a general guideline, I would encourage you to use your veto right only in very rare, extreme cases.

Very often, a new tantric idea might stretch a bit your comfort zone. However, dare to experiment.

As soon as you try, you will notice that you might actually like it a lot.

If your partner is leading, really let go of trying to direct.

SURRENDER!

PLAY THE GAME!

ACCEPT THAT YOUR PARTNER IS IN CHARGE FOR THIS SESSION!

If they suggest a practice, of course don't be there passive asking them to do everything.

Engage! Play! But let them lead!

This is one of the core keys to successful tantric sessions.

It is this ability to lead and be led.

You can alternate the leading role in a session or between sessions.

For instance you can lead for 10 min and then let your partner lead for another 10 min.

Or you can bring in an idea, practice it and let your partner bring in the next idea.

If one of you is way more inspired, has many wishes and the other is comfortable with being led, one partner can keep the leadership role for a few sessions or even all the time IF IT'S SOMETHING YOU BOTH want.

I would say that in most situations, alternating the leadership role is more balanced and gives space and power to each one of you.

Remember that these "technicalities" are something you discuss together before or after a tantric sex session.

Don't fall into the fanaticism or high expectation trap

Tantric sex comes from a place of freedom, not demand or pressure.

Life is already perfect the way it is now.

There is no distant goal to achieve.

You are already holy, sacred and totally fulfilled as a human being.

Tantric sex simply ads flavor, color, pleasure, fun, delight, bliss... to what already exists.

Feeling pressured is a massive turn off to anyone.

If you are in a couple, you must always start from a place of total mutual respect and freedom for each other's choices and preferences.

The fact that you practice tantric sex doesn't give you the right to tell anyone what to do (unless it is simply agreed mutual exploration within a tantric sex session).

What I mean is that putting pressure on your partner will most likely kill the magic instantly.

That's not the way to go at all.

Your partner might not be in the mood or have other priorities.

That's ok! Don't force them!

If you feel that you want to go deeper in tantric sex exploration and are not sure how your partner feels about it, the best is to sit down and have a quick chat about it...

You can say something like: "I feel there are a few tantric sex techniques I would love to explore and was wondering if it is an experience you would like to share too..."
This is an open freeing discussion where you give each other full space to choose what you want.

If your partner is not into these practices at all, you can try to take very small steps together, do some self exploration or find another potential tantric partner.

Yes, tantric sex can be a major life changing set of practices you want to bring into your life.

Yes, it could be a deal breaker in a relationship if you are full on into it and your partner is not.

This type of fundamental difference of views often happens in couples.

Other similar examples could be having children or not, where you want to live, key life style choices, life vision, etc.

When you face a dead end in your couple, always ask yourself the question: is this a deal breaker? Does it justify us splitting up over this?

If it does, then this must not stop you from expressing mutual respect towards each other. This difference of perspectives is all it is: a difference between you and them.

It is ok to be different! Not everyone needs to merge within a given stream.

As I mentioned earlier, tantric sex might be suitable for maybe 10% of people.

It doesn't mean that the other 90% don't have tantric sex potential of course!

It simply means that tantric sex is not for them for reasons like lack of need or interest, other priorities, other belief system, lack of openness, other sexual preferences, lack of time, etc...

Respect their choice at 100% and simply be free to make YOUR own choices too.
Remember that nobody owns another human being and the planet is a much better place when the only thing we truly control is our own life.

Sensual touch with oils

Here is a simple approach to connect with your tantric sex partner.

This technique can be used as foreplay to intimacy, by itself or alternated with other energy building techniques.

Simply sit crossed legged, half lotus or lotus facing each other.

You can be totally naked (ideal), top less or simply with arms and other parts of your upper body naked.

Use some sensual massage oil that you can find in new age shops or from the body shop brand for instance.

Then, simply close your eyes, breathe deeply a few times, relax for a couple minutes in that posture.

The goal now is to touch each other's body in a very gentle way.

In the beginning use only one or two fingers.

Poor a few drops of oil on them and touch your partner's arm, hand and expand to parts of the torso, breasts, shoulders, etc.

One person stays passive and simply enjoys the feelings. You can close your eyes and dive into the delight of having someone take care of you.

After a minute or more, you can alternate and if you have been the one touching, become the passive one.

You can alternate like this a few times and eventually start touching each other's body at the same time.

Keep using your full hand mainly for the end of this tantric session.

Just one or two fingers might be better in the beginning.

You can as well use the top of your five fingers, one hand or both hands.

Feel into it and trust your instinct.

It's not a fixed method ;)

Keep it subtle for a while.

Really! Don't rush!

You have plenty of time.

This builds up lots of sensuality and delight between the two of you.

If you want to intensify this, you can add more oil and start massaging each other's body with the full hand at the same time.

You can then come closer, face to face and let one of the partners sit on the other's person lap.

You will then massage each other's body by playing with your two bodies against each other.

At this stage, this tantric session can of course evolve to higher levels of intimacy if you are open for it but it is always a good idea not to rush, so that the subtle delight and energy built between the two of you has space to expand.

If you engage into a more passionate style, you can as well, go much more wild and let passion take over.

This type of intimacy building creates intense waves of pleasure all over your body.

You discover each other's sensual responses and it is definitely a good thing to do if you want to rebuild intimacy with your partner for instance.

You can as well take pauses, stop half way and stay silent, eyes closed in front of each other, while you dive into a silent meditative moment.

Ad rhythm to this session.

For instance if you focus on touching a woman's breast, stay in that area for a minute before you let her take over and becomes the active one.

Same the other way round, if you touch a men's torso and start gently moving in direction of his lingam, you can approach it gently, lightly strike it just once and move away to build up desire.

If you don't know how long to stay in one area, use a few seconds to a minute as a general idea for your moves.

For instance, you alternate roles like every minute to every few minutes.

If you stretch a move for too long, the energy can slightly drop as well.

This is a dance you improvise and part of you already knows the exact pleasure moves.

Trust your instincts and own this moment.

You are the tantric artist.

Painting art and writing mantras on each other's bodies

As you explore, each other's sensual dimensions here is another direction you can dive into.

You can use some body paint (check in an art or make up shops) and draw beautiful shapes on your partner's body.

You can for instance lie down and let your partner paint on you or the other way round.

You can as well sit facing each other to do that.

Don't cover your whole body with paint of course ;) - Be subtle.

These are like winks of positive energy you give to each other.

It is a way of saying: "I love your body and I decorate it with beauty"

You can as well use sacred powders used in India for bindus. You have them in red, orange and white for instance.

(these are the colors you see saddhus often wearing with all sorts of symbols on their foreheads)

You can take some of that powder, mix it with a tiny bit of water and use your finger or a small brush to initiate your partner's body.

You can as well write words on each other.

Here are some ideas:

- Love
- Delight
- Beauty
- Tantra
- Union
- Peace
- Harmony
- Shakti
- Shiva

- Etc.

You use each other's body as a mantric support and energize each other's body and mind by doing so.

If you want to write names in Sanskrit script go back to my site and check Sanskrit mantras.

You can learn them or directly copy them on your partner's body.

When you write a god or goddess name on your body, it is a way of reconnecting with an absolute universal reality.

Using divine names realigns your mind with a perfect plan and opens new doors of energy through your being.

I would start with just shapes and then, try a word in English.

If your partner likes it, you can then start using a non personified Sanskrit word like shantih.

After that, you can go further by using one of Shiva's or shakti's names for instance.

If for any reason you feel uncomfortable with using a god or goddess name, no problem, ok? ;)

You can stick to shapes and words in English for instance.

They have as well the power to open new energy doors throughout your body.

Ask for permission

This is something to remember with all these practices.

Check with your partner every now and then to see if they like what you do and if you are not going too far.

Be ready to respectfully stop what you are doing if you notice that anything makes them uncomfortable.

To check if they want to go further, you can say:

- Everything ok? - Do you like that?
- Let me know if at any moment you want to stop, ok? - It's important that you feel totally safe
- Is it ok if I touch you with some oil?
- Etc.

Listen, ok?

Always be respectful and give your tantric partner all the space they need if they want to interrupt a session or need to take it more slowly.

Never be pushy or demanding.

Want to play?

Entering the "tantric field" can be very challenging for many.

Why?

Because it unleashes life force in your system.

It is like jumping in a fresh mountain stream and being cleared with new energy.

Yes! Extra life force can be disturbing when you are not used to it.

It can create slight discomfort because it really changes your mind and emotions.

Opening a clear channel of energy between you and someone else means that you get very close to each other.

You see each other without veils.

You need to increase your level of trust and feel strong even though you are totally open.

When you are that open, you might feel vulnerable.

The trick is to be open without losing your power.

That's the challenge!

You can connect on a very intimate level with someone (I don't necessarily mean physical intimacy) without having to feel vulnerable.

Makes sense, right?

Connect!

This is one of the most direct expressions of tantric sex.

In fact there is no sexual expression in it anymore. It is a pure energy connection between you and someone else.

This happens when your life force is awake and flowing.

When you meet someone, there is always a potential exchange of life force, joy and energy.

It happens when you don't hide yourself or don't fear.

When you hold back your energy, it stays unfulfilled.

When you unleash, you connect without pressure or effort.

You notice that energy exchange is the core of that connection.

The key is to unleash and go deeper than the day to day level of communication.

You remove fears or walls and stand "naked" on an energy level.

Of course, your personality is still there. Your desires are still there.

What changes is that there is an extra octave of energy participating in your being and in that exchange.

When this happens you unleash a whole new set of life potentials in the way you relate to others.

Now, your tantric power is an energy you need to master.

When you master it, you generate it, exchange it or direct it at will.

It stays in your being flowing without major effort because it has become your natural state.

Your inner channels are clear and open.

No undigested emotional blocks!

It flows!

You are in harmony with yourself and the planet.

You connect with others in a way which is super effective.

The result is a high level of joy and energy in everything you do.

Magical! Empowering for you and for all those you meet!

Turn any place into a tantric temple

If you go through a typical shopping mall, you won't see many elements reminding you of a tantric temple.

Now, when you master the tantric sex energy, you take it wherever you go.

That's the power which is given to you.

It is so strongly in you that you reflect it in your being and towards others.

Being in a state of Tantra means being alive and feeling connected energy wise with what surrounds you.

It is a state of awareness and high level of flowing energy.

You simply feel that your life force is awake and flowing.

What if you feel challenged by your environment?

What if you have to work in a cubicle and can't get fresh air for a day?

Are you still able to maintain that fresh energy in your system?

How?

Well, you need to regenerate and go back to nature regularly.

Practice tantric sex with your partner.

If you can, simply step out of a limiting environment and simply choose for spaces which reflect your internal state.

What about your house and personal environment?

Can you create a space which reflects tantric power?

Of course you can.

Ask yourself this simple question:

On a scale of 0% to 100%, how alive is your personal space?

If your personal space does not "breathe" it is your job to make it alive!

Yes, you can!

These are probably some of the most empowering steps you can take!

Here are some tips:

- **Add nature, flowers, fresh fruits, etc.**
- **Add streaming water, ponds or fountains.**
- **Choose the right location, peaceful and refreshing.**
- **Ad pictures, mantras, sculptures, calligraphies. Some of my favorites are pictures of Khajuraho and some calligraphy I write myself.**
- **Create beauty. This is one of your key guiding forces: the quest to reflect beauty in you and in your personal space.**
- **Sing and dance. It clears the air.**
- **Clean your space and get rid of clutter. Ad freshness.**
- **Create space!**
- **Marble, crystals, incense, candles.**
- **Etc.**

Okay, these are some of the basics!

Remember that this is more than decorating your personal space.

Any object or element reflects a message.

Think about the objects you choose.

What is their story?

What do they tell you?

When you practice that path, you quickly notice that you develop a "tantric" taste for the way you create your personal space.

One aspect of an object is its esthetical value.

Another aspect is its energy content.

When you engage into tantra, your personal space is your tantric temple.

It is your tantric temple and reflects the tantric energy exactly according to what you put in it.

Don't think that you need to go to some remote tropical forest in India to experience a tantric environment.

You can create and manifest a tantric temple right where you are!

Tantric sex dance!

This is one of the most amazing ways to build up tantric energy between you and your partner.

Choose a nice music, ethnic, mysterious and vibrant.

Get naked and dance, improvise on these beats.

You can touch yourself or touch your partner but in a subtle way.

Don't let passion and excitement take over.

Instead, focus on the beauty of your movements and the play between the two of you.

Play with each other's bodies!

Explore each other's sensuality!

Use your breathing.

Take postures.

Use smiles and a vast diversity of looks towards each other.

This in itself is an amazing tantric sex build up.

The proximity of your bodies will of course trigger sexual tension.

Use kisses and subtle touches. Caress each other's yoni and lingam in very subtle ways.

Let the music and dance take you like a wakeful trance.

If you practiced that with your partner and feel ready for it, you can always invite another experienced couple to your tantric sex dance.

Stay subtle and let the flow of your sensual expression and delight build up in waves of magical fire.

What about energy orgasms?

Even with energy orgasms (without loss of semen for the men), there is still loss of energy and some time to recharge your stamina.

This means that when you engage into tantric sex, it is still better not to go all the way to even an energy orgasm.

You keep on building energy without releasing it.

You will feel the sexual energy building up and opening gates in your being.

You will feel activation of the chakras especially heart and third eye.

Now, if you release energy when building up, you will actually lose precious life force in the process.

Even with an energy orgasm, it can take a few days to rebuild sexual tension.

On the other hand, if you don't release your energy but let it build up, you will put it to much better use.

After a couple of weeks to a month of tantric sex practice, you eventually reach a point where the effects of your practice become extremely present.

Your awareness starts expanding. This is due to the activation of the third eye.

At the same time, you might get this stable feeling of intense joy.

That's the clarification of the solar plexus and the opening of the heart chakra.

Once you reach this energy plateau and break through, having an energy orgasm is somehow much less of a loss of energy.

You maintain that state of sexual tension more easily.

This is as long as you don't orgasm a few times in a row in which case you will lose most of your stamina and get back to your starting point.

The good news is that even if you orgasm and lose energy in the process, you will be able to rebuild energy easily.

Simply give yourself time and be patient as your sexual tension builds up again.

A stream of ecstatic bliss just by being in each other's presence

When your tantric power is awake, that's exactly how it works!

Sensuality streams out of your being and wakes up the same type of sensation in those who are in contact with you.

If you engaged in waking up your tantric energy with your partner, you will feel the tantric aura of desire, sensuality and pleasure all over you for days.

It does not go away! It stays!

It activates your senses and offers you this flow of magical bliss!

This internal feeling simply does not go away for days at a time.

A look or touch from your partner radiates through your whole being.

These waves of fire are pure delight and overpower any other sensual experience.

You feel complete and fulfilled!

You might be longing for more but it is a desire you master and play with.

You can let it go or activate it at will whenever you feel inclined to.

Focus on foreplay for 3 months

When you just met someone, this is what it takes to get familiar with each other's body.

Don't rush into having intercourse.

Instead, focus on play!

Explore physical sensations and let the tantric tension build up until the simplest of your partner's touch wakes up waves of sensual delight.

Imagine how it feels to have all your senses open and awake.

The force waking up these senses and making them super alert is your sexual energy.

If you have intercourse or orgasm before you reach this point of tantric build up, you simply release the flow of energy before it expands in your whole body.

Make it flow and expand in your being by taking time to nurture it with freshness and openness.

Yes! You can stay in these foreplay stages for very long.

Can you build up tantric energy if your partner does not practice it?

Of course you can.

However the impact might be lower than if you are both engaged in it.

When you meet or exchange energy, you end up creating a unified field of energy which is the result of your two inputs.

It is like having a chat with someone. The energy of your conversation will be reflection of what you both put into it.

If your partner engages into sex with a very different idea than yours, you will end up creating something which is more a mixture of sexual attitudes than a pure tantric line.

That's ok of course!

Why? Because sex in itself already has great potential.

When you practice tantric sex, you simply add a new dimension to this natural potential.

Now, imagine that you go sailing with someone who has no clue about it.

How does that feel? You probably end up doing most of the moves, right?

With Tantra, it is the same. It is obviously more fun if you both know how to play.

If your partner is not into tantra at all, there is something you can do though:

Multiply your level of tantric power and overpower their energy.

If you are really good at it, you can guide them in a subtle way.

They will let you take the lead if they can feel you are extremely skilled at what you do.

You need to be directive and gentle at the same time.

It is not control. It is more like mastering and taming the sexual power in both of you.

This could be an entrance door. If your partner feels the impact of your tantric approach, they will want to know more about it and give you space to educate them.

Your tantric skills and tantric power need to be solid though.

Establish a tantric connection with someone you are attracted to

Well, the first step is definitely to make sure you own that energy yourself.

What does it mean?

That you know how to generate, delight, beauty or pleasure any time in your existence if you want to.

See tantric sex energy as a flow of fire you can master and play with.

So, the training is first with you alone.

You need at least a few techniques to freely connect with and master that energy.

Sometimes, this energy will of course spontaneously wake up in you and you will wonder "why now?"

There is always a reason.

Energies follow their own set of laws and balance of forces.

It does not come out of nowhere.

There is always a cause or a source.

Sometimes, it is simply the right time for you and the waking up of the tantric fire is this sudden breakthrough of energy.

Tantric fire is always in you.

Sometimes, it is visible. Sometimes, it is simply overpowered by other forces at play.

Now, back to the question.

Suppose that you have already a high level of mastery of the tantric sex energy.

You see someone and feel this tantric potential with that person.

You feel waves of desire and sensuality.

What do you do? How do you connect?

It is simple: the person you are attracted to will respond if they are touched by the same energy.

This energy is intelligent.

It is a force at play which has its own agenda.

We, as agents are part of this agenda.

Why?

Because we are creators.

It is the role of the energy to instruct us and guide us on how to use that force and play with it.

It is always a trilogy or triangle, never simply the play of two persons.

There is always a third entity or intelligence involved.

You can call this force the tantric sex spirit.

Now, this spirit has its own set of forces and balance.

To create a perfect energetic reaction, you need to find the right posture.

You find this posture on various levels:

- **The right mind set, thoughts and emotions.**
- **The right attitude, vision or plan.**
- **The right action.**

This is not simply an incoherent action line.

There is a clear plan or vision behind this force.

The goal is to reach a total and absolute state of unity.

Of course, the play of sensuality is like a flirt you have with this force.

It takes you in its arms. It nurtures you and activates the fire channels in your being.

You can have a simple glimpse of that energy or a deep break through after days of sensual play.

Once you feel this potential waking up, it magnetizes you totally.

It is one of the big successes you can achieve in this life time:

A total, overwhelming, clear and energizing mystical union or opening.

A simple touch of this experience changes your life forever.

It frees your total being and repositions you as a free universal spirit rather than just someone trying to cope with society's demands.

The goal is not to escape creation.

It is to ad this quality of fire which does free your being forever.

Sex without this connection can have the same type of effect.

However, in my experience, the sponsorship of
this tantric force multiplies the power and extent of a sexual experience.

Keep in mind that right now, we talk about tantric sex, but you can have similar type of experiences without sex being involved.

You can find yourself for instance naked playing in wild ocean waves under the sun and having this incredible feeling of joy. This experience can remove all fears or worries out of your mind and open new doors of total clear awareness.

It is the same type of experience. You simply use another type of action to get there. The energies and experiences can be very similar.

But let's get back to tantric sex.

We now know that there is:

- **A plan.**

- A third entity (besides you and your potential partner) you can call the tantric spirit.

- **A target you can reach.**

Feedback minute

Sometimes your partner will do something that really stimulates a whole new flow of delicious sensations all over your body!

At another moment they might touch you in a way which is not exactly nice.

What do you do?

Do you share your feelings on the spot?

If it's something nice you can of course!

Now, when they are engaged into tantric play, partners might not be open to be educated on something they could do differently.

The best time to give your partner any feedback is the following day or even a couple of days later.

You can say things like:

"It really works for me when you touch me that way"

or

"That created some pain..."

or

"There is something I would like you to try next time if you are open for it..."

Your words will tell them exactly what works for you and what doesn't.

Sometimes, your partner might believe they are touching you in a way you like when in fact you can't stand it!

So to avoid confusion, tell them, share, offer feed back and be open to receive it as well.

It is one of the essential keys to keep on progressing together.

The key is to give feed back when your partner is open for it.

If what you have to say is challenging, warn them and ask them if it is a good moment.

Timing!

Positive feedback is of course much easier to give :)

Sensual massage oils - Olive oil - Body milk - Yogurt - Clay

These are all substances you can use to enhance pleasure and explore new sensations:

- **Sensual massage oils**

There is a good brand in the "body shop". You can as well find them in most new age shops. Get a bottle and cover your chest with it before you rub your bodies against each other. If you are a woman, use this oil as well to massage your partner's lingam. It definitely increases his pleasure and gives you a whole new avenue to stimulate his sexual power.

- **Olive oil**

Use in a moderate way. Try it first to see if you like the smell and feeling.

- **Body milk**

An excellent way to care for each other's bodies. Massage the breasts or chest, belly back legs, inner leg, feet. You can as well cover your whole body with it and go into embrace and even intercourse while rubbing your bodies against each other.

- **Yogurt**

You can use it in small quantities, poor it on a woman's breast to leak. You can as well poor some on a man's lingam to leak as well. If you are up to it, take a liter of liquid yogurt and shower with it while massaging each other's body. It's refreshing and very purifying.

- **Clay**

Another amazing substance. You can buy a package of clay for internal or external use. You can use as well art clay with lots of water. If you are lucky, you can as well find clay in nature for instance on a river bed and cover your body with it while naked in nature.

All these substances have the power to add a new dimension to your tantric sensual experience. Dare to explore, play with them and don't forget to let me know if you find a new one I did not mention yet, ok?

Tantric play in nature

Nature is EXTREMELY conductive for tantric sex energy.

Imagine how it feels, when you are alone with your partner in nature and can engage in short exciting tantric play moments.

As with other contexts, you can let your imagination go wild and explore how the wind or the sun feels on your skin while your partner gives you incredible pleasure.

Dare to play!

Tantric cycles

Somehow, the evening/night seems to be more conductive for tantric sex energy.

It is not exclusive of course.

It seems that during the day, the mind is naturally geared towards more practical tasks.

The evening tends to bring more mystery, refinement, beauty and tantric excitement

Experiment yourself with this and let me know what you discover, ok?

Master your sexual energy

Master your sexual energy

This is one of the key goals of tantric sex.

The second goal is to use your sexual energy to reach a state of absolute unity.

Conclusion

I hope you enjoyed this material!

Feed back? Questions? Success stories?

Email me at francisco@vitalcoaching.com

For coaching:

http://vitalcoaching.com/coaching.htm

For more:

http://vitalcoaching.com

To your power

Francisco Bujan

CPSIA information can be obtained at www.ICGtesting.com
Printed in the USA
BVOW08s1854260215

389523BV00013B/313/P